Symeon Romylos was born in Kozani to parents who came to Greece from Constantinople. After the Athens University of Economics and Business, he pursued further education in the USA, earning an MBA from St. John's University. Upon returning to Greece, he held various roles at Unilever, including organization and methods manager, a two-year stint at their headquarters in Rotterdam, and ultimately serving as the commercial director of Elais-Unilever in Greece. Symeon has contributed numerous letters and articles to Greek financial journals, with over 60 publications in Capital.gr.

Symeon Romylos

The Warren Buffett Paradox and Its Solution

Systems Analysis vs. Economic Theory to End the Tax Avoidance of the Rich

AUSTIN MACAULEY PUBLISHERS™

LONDON • CAMBRIDGE • NEW YORK • SHARJAH

Ordering Information

Quantity sales: Special discounts are available on quantity purchases by corporations, associations, and others. For details, contact the publisher at the address below.

Publisher's Cataloging-in-Publication data

Romylos, Symeon
The Warren Buffett Paradox and Its Solution

ISBN 9798891556171 (Paperback)
ISBN 9798891556188 (ePub e-book)

Library of Congress Control Number: 2024910774

www.austinmacauley.com/us

First Published 2024
Austin Macauley Publishers LLC
40 Wall Street, 33rd Floor, Suite 3302
New York, NY 10005
USA

mail-usa@austinmacauley.com
+1 (646) 5125767

Dedicated to the tax legislators of the world!

This book would not have been written if it had not been preceded by a book published in Greece in 2022, with similar ideas, nor without the help of Bing AI! My acknowledgements to that book end as follows. Finally, I choose to declare that I consider myself lucky to have been in America. This country gave me the unique opportunity to study and work while, later on, Unilever made use of these studies by providing me with substantial, multi-level knowledge that developed into valuable experience. As it is known, "theory without experience is empty, while experience without theory is blind."

Table of Contents

Foreword

What will be discussed in this essay are well-known but necessary points. They describe the problem and its environment so that the proposed solution can be comprehended and accepted. Taxation isn't merely a technical matter; it's primarily a political and philosophical question. Justice in taxation paves the way for social justice.

The tax avoidance of the wealthy was notably underscored by billionaire Warren Buffett as early as 2007, in a renowned interview, when he remarked, "There's been class warfare going on for the last 20 years, and my class has won. We're the ones that have gotten our tax rates reduced dramatically." Since then, he is often cited by various writers or speakers addressing this issue. This is what we have playfully termed "The Warren Buffett Paradox."

During his State of the Union address on February 7, 2023, the US President, Joseph Biden, stated, "it is time for the top 1% and the big corporations to start paying their fair share of taxes," and he concluded, "The tax system is not fair, it's not fair. We're going to change that." Yet the reforms implemented subsequently have not resolved the real problem. To underscore this, in January 2024, 250 of the wealthiest individuals on the planet penned a letter addressed to world leaders meeting in Davos, requesting to be taxed.

As known, the problem is believed to arise because the so-called 'capital income' generated through the possession of wealth, such as rental income, gains from selling shares, dividend income, etc., are taxed at lower rates than wages and salaries, which many economists refer to as 'the fair tax'. In reality, this incorrect tax treatment stems from a failure by economic theory to define the three possible forms of income. Additionally, and more significantly, the profits of corporations are not distributed to the shareholders, to whom they belong, so that they might be legally possible to be taxed with "the fair tax."

A billionaire highlights the existence of a tax paradox. A president of the world's strongest economy acknowledges the existence of this tax paradox. 250 of the wealthiest people on the planet are still advocating to be taxed.

Despite all of the above and much more, no concrete proposals for a realizable solution have emerged. Nevertheless, as will be demonstrated, all the necessary conditions are in place to conclusively rationalize this paradoxical situation, i.e., to eliminate this tax unfairness.

All that is needed is a government decision.

Introduction

The sole purpose of this paper is to address how the Warren Buffett paradox can be solved, and how this tax inequity can be rectified. As will be elucidated below, this can be achieved by distributing the profits of corporations (not necessarily in cash) to the shareholders, and they are taxed with the 'fair tax' alongside all their incomes of the 'first form'.

This is not a tax study or any other form of scientific thesis. It is a systems analysis and redesign of the relevant procedures.

It does not necessitate a lengthy text spanning hundreds of pages, nor does it require citations or references. All data cited are either widely known or available on the internet with the assistance of Bing AI. When text is copied from a source, it is indicated in *italics,* and any emphasis in black is always our own.

Systems analysis serves as a managerial tool for identifying and clearly defining objectives, desired outcomes, and designing systems and procedures to achieve them effectively. It is a problem-solving technique.

In our case, the analysis of the system, in addition to the findings mentioned in the preface, has revealed that the failure to continuously update the rules concerning corporations is the reason why the profits of corporations are not distributed to the shareholders (only 'procedurally') so that they could be legally taxed with the "fair tax." Historical remnants are not uncommon in all systems—legal, taxation, business, etc. For instance, the once permitted anonymity of shares vanished only 'accidentally' due to the dematerialization of all shares!

While we may think we understand what a corporation is, it is necessary for our analysis to point out that the term 'corporation' is one of the most characteristic examples of—to borrow Yuval Noah Harari's eloquent description—*"The truly unique feature of our language is not its ability to transmit information about men and lions. Rather, it's the ability to transmit information about things that do not exist at all."*

As Harari explains, human success was predicated on shared collective myths (such as liberalism, equality, human rights, gods, etc.), i.e., things that do not exist at all. However, human success primarily stemmed from ideas, things that do not exist at all! The fundamental behavioral disparity between humans and other beings is that whenever something impedes progress or the pursuit of goals, humans contrive something that "does not exist," a conceptual aid, such as a 'corporation', and…voilà!

It is imperative not to overlook that all things that 'do not exist' were contrived by humans to aid in achieving objectives. In other words, they are all tools, aids. 'Company' or 'money', just like 'equality' or 'gods', are symbols that convey meanings of such aids. Unfortunately, however, all useful things have more than one utility. The corporation can be—and is de facto used—as a means of tax avoidance…

When we forget this, we perceive the world through distorting lenses.

However, when we examine the fundamentals of the historical evolution of the institution of the 'company', it becomes evident that the conditions and facts that once prevailed no longer hold true. Not taxing shareholders with the 'fair tax' for the profits of their companies is now not only unnecessary but, on the contrary, both undesirable and feasible to change!

Part A.

The Solution of The Paradox, The End of The Inequity

1

The Problem Data

As stated earlier, the two components directly relevant to the issue are what constitutes a company and what constitutes a share.

1.1 What is a company

A company is an organization of people, such as a trade union, a professional chamber, a state, the European Union, or the United Nations. Like any organization of people, it was contrived to achieve something that could not be achieved—or achieved sufficiently effectively—by individuals. Therefore, all of these organizations are tools; they are aids to humans for the achievement of the respective ends that human beings, natural persons, pursue. In every such organization, there are either individuals or organizations of people, and the participants have different responsibilities, different rights, and different obligations.

In corporations, limited liability allows individuals to take risks they would otherwise not venture or would be unable to take. The participation of many shareholders allows the pooling of resources that would be impossible to be raised from a single individual, and the other well-known advantages.

Historically, *early forms of companies that foreshadow the corporation can be traced back to the Middle Ages. However, the history of the société anonym has its essential origins in companies created in the 17th and 18th centuries in the Netherlands, England, and Germany. These were partly private and partly state-owned enterprises, which were instruments of business penetration in countries such as India, America, and other colonies. [...] The East India Company (1603) and the Bank of Amsterdam (1608) are the two models that formed the basis of the institution of anonymity, which was to cause a real revolution in subsequent social and economic development.*

But the anonymity of shares has already been abolished! It is perhaps the perfect example of an institution that has ceased to be useful. It was contrived to facilitate the raising of capital etc., at a time when anonymity was thought to be, or indeed was, a prerequisite for achieving this desired result.

What followed is well known, and it doesn't matter whether it was technology that facilitated the abolition of printing (which is a prerequisite for an anonymous 'title deed', such as a share) or developments in general (money laundering, etc.) that made anonymity itself undesirable. The important thing is that the printed share—a once considered indispensable feature of the corporation—is now no longer necessary. It also matters that it is now socially desirable that the corporation ceases to serve as a tool for tax avoidance, and, as will become apparent below, both the technology and the legal framework in place are perfectly adequate to achieve this goal.

As we have seen, the corporation "does not exist." There are the entrepreneurs and original shareholders, who set up companies, which evolve as they evolve. Both the founders and the subsequent ordinary shareholders do not invest because they can avoid taxes! They have other, much more powerful incentives to do so.

Regarding the taxation of the profits of companies, this started late since laws are enacted to regulate the consequences of acts and relationships that have already occurred. For example:

> *– In Greece, companies (société anonym) were not subject to Income Tax until 1877, when a tax of 2% was imposed for the first time on dividends only.*
> *– In the USA, the federal corporate income tax was first applied in 1909 with a flat rate of 1% for all business income over $5,000.*

After World War II, the prevailing thinking was that the profits of companies that were not distributed should be taxed at lower rates, as an incentive to reinvest in the growth of the economy, and taxed 'additionally' when distributed.

Since then, dividends have not been taxed in a tax-efficient way anywhere, i.e., they are not taxed at the 'fair tax', and the shareholder claiming a tax-credit for the tax paid by the company.

Let us now consider the basic legal characteristics of the institution in modern times. All organizations of people are abstract concepts, which, in order to become distinct entities, with their own rights and obligations, need to be recognized as legal 'persons'. For corporations, irrespective of the legal wording and minor differences that exist in the various countries, in general, the following apply, which are of interest to us:

A corporation is a legal "person," a legal "entity," *separate and distinct from its owners, having many of the legal rights and obligations that natural persons have.*" A separate and distinct entity means that the shareholders are not responsible for the consequences of their company's actions; it is the corporate entity or its management that are responsible for them.

More specifically, concerning the losses of companies, while the shareholders are obligated to bear them, their liability is limited to the amount of their shareholding. This limited liability, following the abolition of anonymity, is the most important common feature of corporations in all legal regimes. However, taxing shareholders for the profits of their companies neither invalidates their limited liability nor does it constitute an assumption of loss in any sense. Under no circumstances is a shareholder to be asked to increase his investment, to pay money to cover any losses of the company.

This, if it is not already the case, will become abundantly clear when we consider the new regime. In addition:

There is no social need or justification for not recognizing some of the 'actions' of legal persons as actions of the corresponding physical persons, provided that this does not impede the achievement of the legitimate aims of the legal person. After all, in all legal regimes, only natural persons are punished for violations of certain kinds committed by legal persons, never the legal persons which, in theory, committed them. Why, when it comes to non-illegal acts, must we refuse to acknowledge that they are committed by natural persons, that legal persons simply 'do not exist'?

Obviously, then, if there is an impediment to shareholders being taxed for their company's profits, and there is one, it only arises from the fact that income tax is levied on earned income. Therefore, in order for the profits of the legal entity to be considered taxable income of the shareholders, it is not enough for these profits to belong to the shareholders, as they indeed belong to them, the shareholders must also acquire them.

But, for tax purposes and the law in general, acquisition does not presuppose receipt. For example, the profit from sales on credit by businesses is considered realized—and therefore taxable income— which is taxed at the time the sale is made, regardless of when the value of the goods sold is received.

Next, we will see how shareholders can acquire the profits of their company without necessarily receiving them in cash.

1.2 What is a company share

Regardless of the fundamental—almost universal in all countries—legal characteristics of the share, it is beneficial to comprehend what it truly represents, why it exists, and the purpose it serves.

Originally, when shares had to be printed, a share was a certificate indicating that the holder *"owns one of the equal parts into which the **share capital** of a company is divided."* However, even then, this only applied at the time of establishing a corporation. Subsequently, the holder of a share was, is, and will be the owner of one of the equal parts into which the **net worth**—not only the share capital—of a company is divided. This remains the value transferred with the sale of a share.

After all, for tax purposes, the value of a business is its net book value, and its taxable profit is the amount by which its net book value increases in a fiscal year.

What this signifies is that when shareholders sell a share, they transfer ownership of value which they somehow ended up owning, even though, procedurally, they **have never 'earned' or 'acquired' it!**

This alone could justify the proposal to tax the shareholders for the profit of their corporation, since they **inevitably** end up owning it.

As is known, all shares without exception have been dematerialized, replaced by electronic records, and, as has been observed, this has had significant collateral advantages! Furthermore, the number of shares, the parts into which the value of a company is divided, can be any number. In practice, companies can and sometimes do increase or decrease the number of shares whenever they deem it desirable.

Therefore, why should the value of a company be divided into other 'parts' since it is already divided into as many parts as the monetary units that define the size of that value? That is, why should a share not represent one monetary unit of net book value of the company? Of course, if necessary for stock exchanges, share 'trading units' can be for a multiple or for a fraction of a monetary unit.

2

The New Regime

In order to tax shareholders for the profits of their corporation, all that is required is to maintain the shareholders' registers as if they were bank accounts with the following terms and conditions:

1.   Interest (the profits) is credited once a year and is linked to the 'bank's' profitability, hence potentially a loss.
2.   There is no right of withdrawals but there is a right to transfer all or part of the account.
3.   The 'bank' has the right to return part of the deposit at its discretion.

As simple as that.

2.1 Shareholders' registers

In the year the new system is introduced, the number of shares in each shareholder account will increase (or decrease) accordingly. For example, a shareholder who has 100 shares, which on 1/1 of the year the new system is introduced had a net book value of $12,3456 per share, will henceforth have 1.234,56 shares, i.e., she/he will receive 1.134,56 new shares. In today's conditions, this is a split of shares at a ratio of 11.3456 new shares for each old one. Nothing in the present regulations prevents it. Thereafter, at the end of each year, the profits will be distributed to the shareholders who will receive one new share at an acquisition cost of $1.00, for every $1.00 of profit attributable to them.

Therefore, a cash distribution (under current practice it would be a return and a reduction of the share capital) would mean a return and a reduction of the net worth with a corresponding reduction of the number of shares. However, because they will receive $1.00 for each canceled share, regardless of the stock market price, in order to avoid possible manipulation of the stock price, cash distributions should be announced well in advance of the day of payment. Possibly, any cash distribution should be required to be made only to shareholders on record as of 12/31.

First, each company will announce the terms of the split, as it is done now. Next, the implementation of the new system will start sometime in the year which will be chosen as the first year of implementation of the new tax regime.

Let us now see an example. To make it easier to follow the reasoning, small, round numbers are used. Of course, in reality, the relative sizes are what they are, but this is not a problem for computers.

Let us suppose that trading the new shares of company ABC will start on 07/01/01. On 01/01/01 (year of the beginning of the new tax regime), the company had a net book value of $1,000 with 200 shares outstanding. Given that the shares must have a value of $1 each, the 200 should become 1,000. Therefore, the 200 will receive 800 or, 1 will receive (800/200=) 4 additional.

Evidently, when the new shares, i.e., the profits are distributed, the shareholders will be taxed on them at the progressive tax scale! Thus, they will be taxed at the 'fair tax'!

The above creates a practical cash flow problem for shareholders who, now, will have to disburse to pay the tax. However, since companies will not be taxed, they will be able to distribute this amount in cash, and/or, since shareholders will receive new shares, they will be able to sell some of them.

As already mentioned, any distribution of cash will mean a return of net worth, which, as is now the case with returns of capital, will not be taxable. Another issue, in this case procedural, arising from the above, is the need for companies to withhold and remit to the tax authorities, tax on incomes earned by foreign tax residents, as is now the case for dividends paid to foreign shareholders. Quite simply, to pay the foreign shareholders' tax, the company may issue fewer shares for these shareholders.

2.2 Accounting for shareholders

What was mentioned in the above example for Company ABC, and what is mentioned below for Shareholder 'A' and Shareholder 'B', are illustrated in the two tables below.

Suppose the aforementioned company has a profit for the year of $100.00. This will be distributed on 03/31/02 to the shareholders on record as of 12/31/01, to the 1,000 existing shares; that is, for every 1 existing share the shareholder will receive (100/1,000=) 0.1 new share. At the same time, cash of $0.01 per share will be distributed.

Shareholder «A»	Shares	Average price	Acquisition Cost	Value of transaction	Profit -Loss
01.01.01 Before the new system	100,00	6,2000	620,00		
07.01.01 New Shares	400,00	0,0000	0,00		
Balance	500,00	1,2400	620,00		
08.30.01 Sale to shareholder B	-100,00	1,2400	-124,00	139,98	15,98
Balance	400,00	1,2400	496,00		
03.31.02 Distribution of profits of year 1	40,00	1,0000	40,00		
03.31.02 Cash didtribution	-4,00	1,0000	-4,00		
Balance	436,00	1,2202	532,00		

On 08/30/01, the second shareholder 'B' purchased 100 shares from shareholder 'A' at $1.45 per share and paid $145.00 plus expenses, totaling $150.75, while shareholder 'A' received $145.00 minus expenses, netting $139.98.

Subsequently, on 09/20/01, shareholder 'B' bought another 50 shares from a third party, shareholder 'X', on the stock exchange, at a total cost (including expenses) of $75.88, or $1.5176 per share. Thus, shareholder 'B' now possesses 100 + 50 = 150 shares with an acquisition cost of $150.75 + $75.88 = $226.63, or $1.5109 per share. These details are shown in table 'B' below.

Shareholder «B»	Shares	Average price	Acquisition Cost	Value of transaction	Profit -Loss
08.30.01 Purchase from shareholder A	100,00	1,5075	150,75	150,75	
09.20.01 Purchase from shareholder X	50,00	1,5176	75,88	75,88	
Balance	150,00	1,5109	226,63		
03.31.02 Distribution of profits of year 1	15,00	1,0000	15,00		
03.31.02 Cash distribution	-1,50	1,0000	-1,50		
Balance	163,50	1,4687	240,13		
05.12.02 Sale	-60,50	1,4687	-88,86	95,67	6.81
Balance	103,00	1,4687	151,27		

On 03/31/02, when the profits of year 01 are distributed, and 0.1 share is given for each existing share, shareholder 'A' has 400 and receives 40 new shares, of course, at a cost of $40.00, and shareholder 'B' has 150 and receives 15 at a cost of $15.00.

The cash distribution of $0.01 per share means that shareholder 'A' receives $4.00 and his number of shares is reduced from 440 to 436, and shareholder 'B' receives $1.50 and his number of shares is reduced from 165 to 163.50.

Finally, suppose that, on 5/12/02, shareholder 'B' sells 60.5 shares, receives $95.67 after deducting expenses and makes a profit of $6.81.

2.3 Various procedural matters

Every state is interested in taxing not only the income earned by its citizens but also the income generated in the country, in this case, the profits of companies in the country, earned by foreign nationals. Usually, these are taxed at rates provided for in Bilateral Tax Agreements. Let us look at the possible cases.

1.   The shareholder is a natural person, a tax resident of the country. Exactly as in the above examples.

2.   The shareholder is a legal person, a tax resident of the country. Exactly the same, except that it increases its own profits, which are distributed to its own shareholders—natural persons. Note that these are profits for the same tax year, so the total is distributed to the shareholders on record as of 12/31.

3.   The shareholder is a foreign tax resident, either a legal or natural person. As already mentioned, (see end 2.1), the company may issue fewer shares for this shareholder and pay his/her/its tax to the IRS.

4.   The shareholder, whether a legal or natural person, is a tax resident of a country with which there is no Bilateral Double Tax Agreement. If a natural person, he/she is taxed accordingly. If it is a legal person, because it could be owned by a resident taxpayer, the tax authorities of the country can act at their discretion. In any case, they will be aware of the fact.

3

The Three Forms of Income

To begin with, and in principle, income refers to the acquisition of value (purchasing power), which, when reduced by the cost of its acquisition—i.e., by any expenditure necessary for its acquisition—becomes taxable income. In theory, this is obvious, and this is how the taxable income of enterprises is calculated. In practice, determining what expenditure is necessary is not always clear. Particularly, the determination of what expenditure is necessary to obtain income from labor, from the actions of humans, is literally impossible.

But first, let us examine the forms of income. There are three forms of income: First Form: the income is part of new (added) value produced in a production process. Second form: the income comes from redistribution, i.e., what one person gains, another is deprived of. Third form: the income comes from surplus value, i.e., an increase in the value of an asset without any expenditure by its owner. Obviously, there are respective losses of value.

Incomes of the First Form are those that come from and are part of new value that is produced (added) in a production process, and the recipients of this part earn it as compensation for some contribution of theirs to the production of this value. Specialization and division of labor, the complexity of methods, institutions, aids, etc., etc., involved in modern production processes (primary, secondary, or even tertiary) often make it indistinguishable both who contributes what and, as just mentioned, what is the cost of acquisition, i.e., the expenditure necessary to obtain what is contributed, be it labor, capital, or aids in lieu of labor or capital. We shall explore this further later when we delve into how value is produced—a subject on which confusion often prevails. For the moment, it is noted that new value is produced (added) only by humans. Inanimate things and abstract concepts such as 'enterprise' contribute, are aids, but they themselves produce nothing nor act otherwise.

Of these three possible forms of income, only the incomes of the first form should be taxed uniformly and cumulatively at the 'fair tax', since only these—but all of them—are compensation for some contribution to the production of new (added) value. In fact, only them and all of them should be those the IRS calls 'earned' income. For example, interest is 'earned income' since this money is contributed via the banking system to some production process. (Or used in the tertiary production process of bank services)

As just mentioned, in reality, whether labor, capital, or aids are contributed, they are contributed by natural persons, even if a legal person may intervene procedurally. Therefore, all incomes of the first form are incomes from actions of humans, i.e., from labor, since they do not come from redistribution, nor from surplus value, nor from any other unknown form of income.

It should be noted that taxing income from all sources of the first form with the 'fair tax' favors low incomes! For example, a low-wage earner or unemployed person with some income from dividends (now from profits) will not be taxed at all.

Part B.

A Few Words About Value

Value is the fundamental concept in economics. Understanding its essence—is pivotal to comprehending what it is, how it is determined, produced, acquired and consequently, how it should be taxed.

As mentioned in the Introduction, there exists a significant degree of confusion on this matter, and clarification may prove beneficial to those engaged in this domain. In this section, we endeavor to clarify some value-related issues through the lens of systems analysis.

The first value-related issue is how value is determined. As is known, one of the most well-known theories is the labor theory of value, which holds that *"the economic value of a good or service is determined by the total amount of socially necessary labor required to produce it."* This theory was developed by classical economists such as Adam Smith, David Ricardo, and Karl Marx.

This theory is correct except that it does not explain how the value of *the total amount of socially necessary labor* can be determined. Adam Smith realized this fact when he tried to solve the water-diamond paradox.

The water-diamond paradox, also known as the diamond-water paradox, is a famous economic conundrum that Adam Smith, the father of modern economics, pondered but was unable to solve. Smith noted that even though life cannot exist without water and can easily exist without diamonds, diamonds are, pound for pound, vastly more valuable than water.

For our analysis we accept that *"the value of any object is not determined by the amount of resources and labor used to create it, but varies according to the context and perspective of its users, determined by the individual who buys or sells it."* This definition has found advocacy in the Subjective Theory of Value and the Theory of Marginal Utility.

4

What is Value

As noted in the preface, determining which incomes can be subject to the 'fair tax' requires establishing the 'forms' of income. However, income and tax concepts are expressed as measures of value in a currency, such as the USD, so it is beneficial to clarify what value is, how it is produced, in addition to how it is determined.

It is acknowledged that different *schools of economic thought offer various theories of value and measures of value.* For our analysis, we adopt the following definition of what value is:

"In economics, value describes the importance of a good for the satisfaction of human needs and its ability to be exchanged with other goods. Measure of the value of a good or a provided service is the price, economic terms that should not be confused."

This means that only exchange value, measured by price (the '*monetary expression of exchange value*'), can be quantified, while real value, i.e., *"the importance of a good for the satisfaction of human needs,".* cannot be measured.

For example, if a thirsty person in the desert pays $100 for a bottle of water, the price paid and the value *it holds for satisfying needs may align.* However, the magnitude of this value remains uncertain, as it is subjective and context-dependent. That is to say, price is a measure of value that arises only after the transaction has taken place and, even then, the magnitude of the value (the "importance…") remains unknown, since we cannot know whether that person would be willing to pay even more, Hence, let's start from the beginning.

Value, for humans has anything useful for achieving or avoiding desired outcomes. Anything devoid of usefulness serves no purpose and holds no value of any kind. (intrinsic, utility or exchange). Of any kind, i.e. none of the 3 intrinsic, utility or exchange value. Satisfying a need equates to satisfying a desire, making value the attribute of tangible or intangible things that meets human needs, from the most urgent to the simplest. This attribute, inherent in goods regardless of their exchange value, constitutes their utility value. This is what value is.

While the value of useful things is intrinsic, in order to be realized, i.e., to 'acquire' utility, these things must be in the possession of users. A diamond in the ground or an apple on an apple tree, cannot satisfy any needs. This acquisition typically occurs through human labor, utilizing tools and aids.

Exchange value, on the other hand, reflects the goods' equivalency, with money serving as the facilitating medium. Thus, goods with utility value generally possess exchange value, although exceptions exist, such as, e.g., souvenirs with utility value limited to their owners.

The concept 'measure' of value, that is price, is a concept that is both conventional and fluid.

It is conventional, because it's a result of societal agreement to consider two goods exchanged to be of equal value. But given that *"value characterizes the importance that a good has for the satisfaction of human needs,"* we cannot conclude, e.g., that a meal, a ticket to a concert, and a tie, all of equal price (exchange value) have equal importance or cause equal satisfaction.

It is fluid because it is subjective. *"It varies according to the context and perspective of its users."*

In conclusion, all goods serve as stores of value, capable of being consumed immediately or stored for future needs. The intricacies of pricing, influenced by factors like competition or uniqueness, aren't necessary to delve into comprehensively here.

5

A Few Words About Needs

As we've just observed, value for human beings encompasses whatever is useful to them, enabling them to achieve or avoid desired outcomes, thereby satisfying needs. This ranges from the most urgent necessities to simple preferences.

It's widely acknowledged that human actions are driven by motivation—a fundamental aspect of our nature shared with all living beings. While the human species has evolved complex needs, the underlying principle remains the same: every action serves to fulfill a need, whether innate or acquired, obvious or inexplicable.

This implies that there are no universally applicable incentives; however, specific incentives generally evoke similar responses from the majority of people. Maslow's hierarchy of needs illustrates this concept, with basic survival needs being largely consistent across individuals, while higher-level needs for self-actualization vary depending on cultural and societal factors.

Yuval Noah Harari further explores the unique human capacity to believe in abstract concepts, such as nations, gods, and money, which form part of our collective myths, shaping our perception of the world.

This ability to believe in nonexistent entities has profound implications for human behavior. While individuals may prioritize their own survival above all else, they are willing to sacrifice their lives for abstract ideals or beliefs. The fulfillment of duties to higher ideals, such as God, country, or family, can evoke boundless satisfaction and joy. Ultimately, the specifics of how needs evolve or are satisfied are less significant than the underlying motivation they provide. Even seemingly irrational economic behavior is driven by the pursuit of need satisfaction.

For instance, the willingness to pay exorbitant sums for items like paintings, often based on their authenticity, underscores the role of belief and perception in value attribution.

Lastly, a very interesting need is the need of risk-taking as it produces economic results that are usually misinterpreted. As we will see below, those who contribute capital to a production process contribute risk-taking, i.e. they contribute the factor of production…'labor'!

6

How Value is Produced

We've observed that value or usefulness, while abstract, holds significance for humans, perceived solely through imagination rather than direct sensory stimulation. In essence, what is produced are not value or usefulness per se, but rather the distinct attributes intrinsic in goods or services, enabling them to fulfill diverse needs.

The preceding discussion on the production of incomes of the first form offers a concise overview of how value is produced. In fact, value for humans—what proves beneficial in fulfilling their needs—is a product of human actions, not solely limited to **labor** (with the meaning given to 'labor' as the factor of production.)

While inanimate objects or abstract concepts lack agency in value creation, they serve as tools or aids, contributing to the production process. Human ingenuity continually devises and employs new tools or aids to enhance efficiency in various pursuits.

Humans, with their actions, draw from (the factor of production) **nature** what it offers for free, using for this purpose material and/or immaterial aids, i.e., (the factor of production) **capital.**

Therefore, if the analysis had to be continued in terms of 'the factors of production', then these factors should be **labor,** meaning anything humans do to produce useful things, **nature** (not land!) from which all it offers is drawn, and **aids.**

What is a factor is one thing and how it contributes to the achievement of an outcome, in this case the production of (added) value, is another. Capital is the result of past production processes, value already produced. **New value is produced (added) by transforming capital with labor.**

Labor is defined as *"physical or mental effort or activity for the production or accomplishment of a desired result."* Therefore, everything and anything humans *do for the production or accomplishment of a desired result is done with physical or mental effort or activity,* that is with **labor.** Consequently, if this is true for everything it is true when the desired result is production of value.

Obviously, both physical and mental effort or activity have different attributes, e.g., fatigue, discomfort, knowledge, skills, talents, etc., etc.

Some of these characteristics are related to mental work and some to physical work. But, except for instinctive reactions, every physical effort or activity is preceded by mental effort or activity, that is, it is preceded by a 'decision'. Therefore, any desired result that requires the use of ideas, information, or knowledge, is accomplished by (the factor of production) labor.

The decision is an invisible 'desired result' of the invisible mental work. One possible decision is to take a risk therefore risk-taking is the result of mental labor, but labor nevertheless. Consequently, the compensation of the contributor of capital to a production prosses is compensation for assuming the risk of losing the value one contributes for temporary use, that is, it is compensation for contributing labor.

The concept is indeed difficult to comprehend. However, in the course of production processes there are many cases where the decision to do absolutely nothing results in the production (addition) of greater value.

By definition, labor is also all services, even if procedurally, they are contributed by legal persons or other legal entities that 'do not exist'.

The decision of risk-taking is of particular interest.

For example, companies charge their production costs with any premiums they pay to insurance companies. But the 'contribution' of the insurance companies, as long as the undesirable does not occur, is one of those things that "do not exist at all," and has no effect whatsoever on the properties of the goods produced.

Exactly the same is the case with the contribution of the relevant services of the state or all of, e.g., the services of the UN. The insurance companies are compensated with the premiums, which are direct costs of production, the states and the organizations of organizations such as the UN are compensated with taxes.

Ignoring the indirect but absolutely necessary contribution to value production by all human organizations, e.g., chambers of commerce or other professional associations, states, as well as by organizations of organizations of humans, e.g. the U.N., is yet another reason that shows how timely the need to rewrite the economic textbooks might be, at least about how value is produced. To this end, it might be helpful to start with the idea of the classical economists that the source of value is labor.

The above mean that there are no 'capital incomes' or 'property incomes' in the current sense of these terms. As we have seen, all incomes of the first form, i.e. those being part of **new value** produced (added), are compensation for a human action, i.e., contribution of **labor,** more and more often mental labor, but labor nevertheless.

Ultimately, every cost incurred in a production process is someone else's gross income, while the net income or profit is the new value produced (added) serving as taxable income.

7

On Ambiguities and Misconceptions Continued

Let's commence with the fundamental question that initiates every system analysis: What is the purpose, the goal, the intended result of economics?

According to Bing AI:

"The purpose of economics is to help people understand the world around them and better respond to the threats and opportunities that arise when things change. The science of economics helps us understand people, businesses, markets, and governments and better respond to the threats and opportunities that arise when something changes. In addition, economics helps us understand the consequences of the decisions we make in our daily lives and in society as a whole."

However, to the question "How does it do all that?" it answers: *"The science of economics studies the production, distribution, and consumption of goods and services in society."*

Thus, while economics delves into what people do to produce what they need to satisfy their needs, its conclusions serve to "help people understand the world around them!" Consequently, it's imperative that the study is comprehensive and the conclusions are valid, as any error could have multifaceted consequences.

Continuing with Bing AI: How is value produced?

"According to economic theory, value is produced in several ways. One of the most well-known theories is the labor theory of value, which holds that

the economic value of a good or service is determined by the total amount of socially necessary labor required to produce it. This theory was developed by classical economists such as Adam Smith, David Ricardo, and Karl Marx."

....

"However, there are other theories that explain the production of value. For example, according to the theory of the cost of producing value, the price of an object or situation is determined by the sum of the cost of the resources used to produce it. Costs can include any of the factors of production, such as labor, capital, or land, as well as **taxation.**

These are just a few examples of how economic theory explains the production of value. Different schools of economic thought have different theories of value and different measures of value."

These are 'just a few examples'…!

Ambiguities and misconceptions about the factors of production

Factor Land

In my first encounter with economics, the factors of production were labor, nature (not land), and capital. Nature is defined as:

"The totality of plant and animal organisms (flora and fauna), geological formations (mountains, soil, subsoil, seas, lakes, etc.), material elements (air, fire, water, etc.) and, in general, **the material universe** *and its functions, considered independently of man, for whom it constitutes the natural environment in which he lives, grows and dies."*

It remains unclear when and why nature morphed into land, construed as 'a piece of ground'. Nature is a factor of production as everything derived from primary production emanates from it. Perhaps the (erroneous) rationale lies in the notion that products of nature come at no cost, being nature's gifts, and thus were disregarded or…forgotten!

Moreover, land, even in the sense of "a piece of ground," isn't merely a factor but an integral component of *the natural environment in which man lives, grows, and dies.*

Possibly due to the pragmatic necessity to acknowledge property rights over land, these parcels acquired exchange value, signifying a cost of acquisition, leading proponents of the theory of the cost of producing value to isolate it from nature.

But land, when bought, should not differ from all assets purchased with capital, such as plants, etc., none of which is recognized singularly as a factor of production.

Furthermore, assets acquired with capital become inputs to the production process and eventually cease to exist. Fixed assets become inputs gradually as they depreciate, ultimately ceasing to exist, also. Conversely, land's cost isn't depreciated as it doesn't wear out; it persists indefinitely.

The fact that land is purchased may have prompted the erroneous acknowledgment that land differs from other fixed assets, which it does, but only for reasons explained above and those to be discussed in Chapter 9 regarding surplus value.

Therefore, there is no production factor called 'land'. The second factor of production is nature, not land.

'Factor' Taxation

According to one theory, *"**costs** can include any of the factors of production, such as labor, capital, or **land** [!!!], as well as **taxation.**"*

Taxation indeed constitutes a cost of any production process, akin to any other cost, passed on to the prices of products or services, and thus borne by consumers, the buyers. This holds true for all indirect taxes and is common knowledge among those involved in related matters.

It is also recognized that direct taxes, levied on the income or property of natural or legal persons and remitted to the State by those individuals, are not shouldered by consumers. However, a misconception persists in this regard, particularly concerning income taxes, whether levied on natural or legal persons. Ultimately, regardless of the payer, they function as a production cost and operate akin to indirect taxes.

Let's start with the evidence. For enterprises, the cost comprises the gross remuneration disbursed to employees. Thus, when employees incur any amount of income tax, this cost is already factored into the prices of the produced goods.

Employees, along with all individuals engaging in activities related to their income, do so based on their after-tax income. The uncertainty regarding the exact amount of tax does not deter them from spending or planning, knowing it will be imposed.

Similarly, businesses (i.e., the natural persons, the managers who strategize and decide accordingly) operate under the assumption that their targeted profit is after taxes. Beyond the inherent logic of this conclusion, specific practices in enterprises substantiate this point:

During the assessment of potential investments, using any criterion (DCF yield, payback period, etc.), the expected profit is always considered after tax. If the anticipated return falls short of expectations, the investment is typically not pursued. This rationale extends to the evaluation of existing investments, and thus the targeted profit, along with pricing policies, is consistently envisioned post-tax.

Certainly, this does not imply that individuals or entities subject to income taxes are unaffected by them or indifferent to their magnitude. Nonetheless, tax equity is a route to social justice, emphasizing the importance of clarifying the function of any tax.

The... Fourth Factor

Another misconception, originating from the classical understanding of labor, is the notion that entrepreneurs do not engage in work!

This notion leads to a cascade of incorrect conclusions. Aside from the ramifications outlined below, it also necessitates another erroneous assumption, with comparable consequences: that value is generated only when the product is intended for exchange or sale, not for self-consumption or proprietary use.

However, this assertion does not withstand scrutiny. Consider someone painting a room. This act fulfills the need of the room's occupants, irrespective of who performs it; thus, the painting constitutes value production regardless of the performer.

Subsequent to the classical era, economists, in their attempts to comprehend or interpret value production, scrutinize the contemporary world and deduce that the three factors—labor, land (replacing nature!), and capital—are insufficient, necessitating the identification of a fourth factor of value production. To this day, economists propose various concepts in search of this elusive fourth factor.

During the post-World War II era, when management saw significant growth and development, some posited 'management' as the fourth factor. Later, 'information' was suggested as another candidate. Presently, 'entrepreneurship' is often touted as the fourth factor of production…!

Presumably, those who advocate for 'entrepreneurship' as the fourth factor perceive it as more significant than the salaried labor provided by a large company's CEO; otherwise, why distinguish it from labor? However, which contributes more value: the entrepreneur who establishes and operates a small convenience store, or the 'salaried' CEO of a multinational corporation? Moreover, at what business scale does one transition from being an 'entrepreneur' to a mere 'manager', and what term encompasses the endeavors of 'small' entrepreneurs?

Moreover, if some advocate for management rather than entrepreneurship as the fourth factor of production, where does one draw the line between an unskilled worker and a CEO?

In general, given the rapidly evolving economic and social landscapes, novel concepts continually emerge, such as the 'knowledge economy' and 'information economy'. However, as previously noted, except for instinctive reactions, every physical endeavor (i.e., work) is preceded by mental effort (also work)—a 'decision' to act or abstain—which constitutes invisible 'desired results' arising from invisible mental labor.

Hence, any desired outcome necessitating the utilization of information, knowledge, or mental acuity is achieved through mental labor, albeit still 'labor'.

8

A Few Words About Redistribution

Redistribution involves the transfer of value, income, or wealth from one or more persons to other(s). It does not entail the production of new value. Redistribution occurs through various social mechanisms, including charity, alimony, indemnity, gambling, insurance, stock markets, taxation, and others. Participation in redistributive mechanisms can be voluntary or forced, sought after or accepted as inevitable by individuals.

These mechanisms are systems, and any interaction with them necessitates a clear definition of objectives: what is sought, why, and what the desired outcomes are.

Inevitable redistribution of value, income, or wealth also happens when the cost of a service provided to many must be shared among them. For instance, taxpayers do not derive equal value from every service provided by states, and it is impractical to tax each citizen separately based on their usage of government services. Consequently, tax systems inherently become redistributive systems.

Additionally, there are mechanisms, such as those encountered during consumer transactions, in which individuals participate unknowingly. Every unit of product produced in a production process bears the same production cost, yet they are not always sold to consumers at uniform prices. Product promotions, for example, aim for an average price, meaning some consumers cover the cost of discounts from which others benefit.

These examples serve as food for thought rather than an exhaustive study of redistribution. Similarly, the following discussion on surplus value exemplifies an approach to addressing problems as systems.

9

A Few Words About Surplus Value

Surplus value is generally defined as *"any increase in the price, i.e., the (exchange) value of an asset, which arises without any expense to its owner, such as an increase in the value of a property near which public utility works were executed, of a piece of land included in the urban plan, of an old object due to collector's trend, etc."*

It's crucial to remember that the value of all goods depends solely on the relation of supply and demand at the moment of exchange, i.e., at the moment of purchase and sale. Therefore, the first question in any similar case should be: "what has changed this relation?"

For instance, how did the execution of *'public utility works'* change this relation? It's evident that these works improve the quality of the estates, altering their properties to make them more useful, thereby satisfying either different needs or the same needs but more effectively. Consequently, the residents of these properties derive greater benefit from their use.

It's worth noting that, especially for residences, their value and usefulness are not solely determined by the properties of the residences themselves. Proximity to schools, shops, public transport stations, etc., adds useful properties, thereby increasing their value. The properties of a seaside plot differ from those of a city center plot, and so on.

Many economists or 'leftist' politicians cite rising property prices as almost irrefutable proof of unjust enrichment, but this is only true in some cases. The main argument supporting the case of unjust enrichment is that an increase in the price of the land a residence sits upon does not justify a corresponding increase in the price of the residence.

As we've discussed, surplus value, i.e., an increase in the price of assets without any expense to their owners, may occur due to a change in the relation of supply and demand. This change can arise from changes in the properties that make an asset useful (e.g., public utility works) or changes in the environment (e.g., construction of a shopping center nearby, changes in interest rates).

Consider two possibilities: if the change in the relation between supply and demand and the increase in land prices resulted from executed works that improved the properties, then the improvement had a cost, borne by taxpayers. In this case, there's a redistribution of value from taxpayers to landowners.

Alternatively, if the increase in real estate prices resulted from a celebrity moving into the area, changing the environment and influencing the qualities—and prices—of houses, this demonstrates how external factors can affect property values.

Moreover, it's known that the value of land tends to increase as cities grow, altering the relation between supply and demand. Additionally, demand for homes fluctuates with changes in interest rates.

Another argument in support of the case of unjust enrichment comes from those who believe that so-called 'capital income' (dividends, rents, and interest) is 'passive' and not produced by work. However, we've established that all dividends, rents, and interest are income of the first form, originating from new value produced in a production process.

Epilogue

As stated in the introduction, the sole intention of this paper is to demonstrate how the Warren Buffett paradox can be resolved and how tax inequity can be eliminated. I believe this goal has been achieved; it was shown that all the conditions are in place to change the tax regime accordingly.

The proposed new tax regime, which taxes corporate profits and incomes of the first form, illustrates how this can be accomplished. All that is needed is a decision by the government.

Regarding the thoughts added in Part B, while I initially intended only to clarify the misidentifications leading to incorrect tax treatments mentioned in the preface, as I proceeded with the analysis, I realized that significant ambiguities and misconceptions prevail in current conceptions about value. I believe that my clarifications are correct and useful.

I imagine that if an economist reads and accepts these findings, s/he may well develop them into a scientific treatise of hundreds of pages and claim the Nobel Prize in economics for the one, single, and unique theory of what is, but mostly, how value, income, or wealth are produced. The subject is simple in its essence: what any being on our planet does to survive, to satisfy its needs.

What makes it complex is the fact that this being is humans, who have contrived and are continually contriving more and more complex, imaginative ways, procedures, tools, generally, material and immaterial aids, in order to become more and more effective, so that they can fulfill their aspirations with the least "physical or mental effort or activity," i.e., labor, as well as the least use of any resources.